How Does My Home Work?
Garbage and Recycling

Chris Oxlade

Chicago, Illinois

www.capstonepub.com
Visit our website to find out more information about Heinemann-Raintree books.

To order:
☎ Phone 800-747-4992
💻 Visit www.capstonepub.com
to browse our catalog and order online.

©2013 Heinemann Library
an imprint of Capstone Global Library, LLC
Chicago, Illinois

All rights reserved. No part of this publication may be reproduced or transmitted in any form or by any means, electronic or mechanical, including photocopying, recording, taping, or any information storage and retrieval system, without permission in writing from the publisher.

Edited by Daniel Nunn, Rebecca Rissman, and Catherine Veitch
Designed by Joanna Hinton-Malivoire
Picture research by Elizabeth Alexander
Production by Alison Parsons
Originated by Capstone Global Library Ltd
Printed and bound in China by Leo Paper Products

16 15 14 13 12
10 9 8 7 6 5 4 3 2 1

Library of Congress Cataloging-in-Publication Data
Oxlade, Chris.
  Garbage and recycling / Chris Oxlade.—1st ed.
      p. cm.—(How does my home work?)
   Includes bibliographical references and index.
   ISBN 978-1-4329-6566-2 (hb)—ISBN 978-1-4329-6571-6 (pb) 1. Refuse and refuse disposal—Juvenile literature. 2. Recycling (Waste, etc.)—Juvenile literature. I. Title.
   TD792.O95 2013
   363.72'8—dc23   2011038249

Acknowledgments
We would like to thank the following for permission to reproduce photographs: © Capstone Publishers p. 23 (Karon Dubke); Alamy p. 18 (© Realimage); Corbis p. 11 (© Image Source); Getty Images p. 21 (Will Heap/Dorling Kindersley); iStockphoto pp. 5 (© Dori OConnell), 15 (© BanksPhotos), 23 (© BanksPhotos); Photolibrary pp. 4 (Corbis), 12 (Jochen Tack/Imagebroker.net); Shutterstock pp. 6 (© Adisa), 7 (© David W. Leindecker), 8 (© HomeStudio), 9 (© tkemot), 10 (© Morgan Lane Photography), 13 (© Tomo Jesenicnik), 14 (© Picsfive), 16 (© MADDRAT), 17 (© Rehan Qureshi), 19 (© Evgeny Karandaev), 19 (© Givaga), 20 (© Jaimie Duplass), 23 (© Tomo Jesenicnik), 23 (© Morgan Lane Photography), 23 (© mikeledray).

Cover photograph of a recycle sign on a recycle bin reproduced with permission of Alamy (© Peter Carroll). Background photograph of plastic bottles reproduced with permission of Shutterstock (© alterfalter).

Back cover photographs of (left) landfill reproduced with permission of Shutterstock (© Picsfive), and (right) a garbage truck reproduced with permission of Shutterstock (© Tomo Jesenicnik).

Every effort has been made to contact copyright holders of material reproduced in this book. Any omissions will be rectified in subsequent printings if notice is given to the publisher.

We would like to thank Paul Mocroft for his invaluable help in the preparation of this book.

Disclaimer
All the Internet addresses (URLs) given in this book were valid at the time of going to press. However, due to the dynamic nature of the Internet, some addresses may have changed, or sites may have changed or ceased to exist since publication. While the= author and Publishers regret any inconvenience this may cause readers, no responsibility for any such changes can be accepted by either the author or the Publishers.

Contents

What Is Garbage? 4
What Is Wrong with Garbage? 6
What Materials Are in Garbage? 8
Why Do We Have Separate Bins for
   Some Garbage? 10
What Happens to Garbage After It Is
   Taken Away? 12
Why Don't We Bury All Our Garbage? 14
Why Do We Recycle Materials? 16
How Much Garbage Do We Throw Away? . . 18
How Can We Throw Away Less? 20
Make a Recycling Tally 22
Glossary 23
Find Out More 24
Index 24

Some words are shown in bold, **like this**. You can find them in the glossary on page 23.

What Is Garbage?

Garbage is all the stuff we do not want in our homes anymore.

Bags and boxes that things are wrapped in are one type of garbage.

The food we do not eat is garbage.

Vegetable peelings and empty cans are garbage, too.

What Is Wrong with Garbage?

Garbage makes a mess if people do not throw it in a trash can.

It spoils the countryside and our streets.

Some garbage has harmful materials in it, which can hurt or kill animals.

Sometimes animals can get trapped by garbage.

What Materials Are in Garbage?

The garbage from our homes contains different materials.

The paper and cardboard in this photograph are from old food packets.

8

Plastic garbage comes from plastic bags, bottles, and food containers.

Other materials found in garbage are glass, metal, food, and garden waste.

Why Do We Have Separate Bins for Some Garbage?

We can **recycle** paper, cardboard, glass, food cans, and some types of plastic.

Recycling means turning garbage into something new that we can use again.

This can is for any garbage that we cannot recycle.

We put things such as diapers and food containers we cannot clean in this bin.

What Happens to Garbage After It Is Taken Away?

Special trucks collect garbage and recycling from our homes.

The trucks also take materials from recycling bins to a **recycling center**.

Garbage that cannot be **recycled** is put into a big hole in the ground.

The place where the garbage is buried is called a **landfill**.

Why Don't We Bury All Our Garbage?

Burying garbage uses up land.

Burying all our garbage also wastes materials that we could **recycle**.

incinerator

Some garbage is burned instead of being buried.

It is put onto a giant fire inside a container called an **incinerator**.

Why Do We Recycle Materials?

recycling symbol

Recycling means that not so much garbage is buried in **landfills**.

When you see this sign, it tells you the material can be **recycled**.

This girl's top is made from recycled material.

Making things from recycled materials means we can use fewer new materials.

How Much Garbage Do We Throw Away?

Each day, a person in the United States throws away about 3 pounds of garbage.

That is as heavy as a child's metal scooter!

Every year, a family of 4 people throws away about 500 glass bottles and jars.

They also throw away about 1,000 cans and 400 plastic bags.

How Can We Throw Away Less?

Stop! Do not throw things that can be **recycled** into a normal garbage can.

Put them aside to be collected, or take them to your local **recycling center**.

You can also **reuse** some things instead of throwing them away.

Yogurt cups make good plant pots!

Make a Recycling Tally

How much garbage does your family **recycle** in a week? List the items below. Then, ask your family to make a **tally** mark each time they put an object in the recycling bin.

Recycling Tally

- Glass bottles and jars ||||| |||
- Plastic bottles |||
- Food cans ||||| |
- Newspapers/magazines ||||| ||||| ||

Glossary

incinerator container or building that holds a fire for burning garbage

landfill place where garbage is buried underground

recycle turn garbage into something new that can be used again

recycling center place where you can take materials to be recycled

reuse use a thing again instead of throwing it away

tally record kept so that you can work out the total of something

Find Out More

Books
Fix, Alexandra. *Reduce, Reuse, Recycle: Paper*. Chicago: Heinemann Library, 2008.

Guillain, Charlotte. *Help the Environment: Reusing and Recycling*. Chicago: Heinemann Library, 2008.

Website
www.epa.gov/students/games.html
Play fun and educational games on this website. Click around to learn more about how you can help the environment.

Index

bags 4, 9, 19
bottles 9, 19, 22
cardboard 8, 10
food 5, 8, 9, 10, 11, 22
glass 9, 10, 19, 22
landfill 13, 16, 23
paper 8, 10

plastic 9, 10, 19, 22
recycle 10, 11, 12, 13, 14, 16, 17, 20, 22, 23
recycled material 17
recycling center 12, 20, 23
reuse 21, 23